American Lives

Eileen Collins

Elizabeth Raum

Heinemann Library
Chicago, Illinois

© 2006 Heinemann Library
a division of Reed Elsevier Inc.
Chicago, Illinois

Customer Service 888-454-2279
Visit our website at www.heinemannlibrary.com

Designed by Joanna Hinton-Malivoire and Q2A Creative

Printed in China by
WKT Company Limited

10 09 08 07 06
10 9 8 7 6 5 4 3 2 1

Library of Congress Cataloging-in-Publication Data
Raum, Elizabeth.
   Eileen Collins / Elizabeth Raum.-- 1st ed.
   p. cm. -- (American lives)
   Includes bibliographical references and index.
   ISBN 1-4034-6943-1 (hc) -- ISBN 1-4034-6950-4 (pb)

   1. Collins, Eileen (Eileen Marie), 1956---Juvenile literature. 2. Women air pilots--United States--Biography--Juvenile literature. 3. Women astronauts--United States--Biography--Juvenile literature. 4. Airpilots--United States--Biography--Juvenile literature. 5. Astronauts--United States--Biography--Juvenile literature. I. Title. II.Series.

   TL789.85.C63R38 2005
   629.45'0092--dc22

                    2005006252

Acknowledgments
The author and publishers are grateful to the following for permission to reproduce copyright material: Alamy Images p. **5** (Andre Jenny); City of Elmira Website p. **7** (Rose Collins. With thanks to Josh Miller); Corbis pp. **6, 8, 9, 10, 11, 12, 16** (John H. Clark); Corbis/Bettmann pp. **14, 15**; Corbis/Reuters p. **17**; Empics/AP Photos p. **18**; Getty Images/AFP p. **19**; Getty Images/Hulton Archive p. **20**; NASA/Dryden Flight Research Center Photo Collection p. **21**; NASA/Johnson Space Center pp. **22, 23, 24, 25, 26, 27**; NASA/Kennedy Space Center cover, title page, pp. **28, 29**; Science Photo Library p. **4**.

Every effort has been made to contact copyright holders of any material reproduced in this book. Any omissions will be rectified in subsequent printings if notice is given to the publisher.

The author thanks Commander Eileen Collins for reading and verifying the material in this book. The author also thanks Doug Peterson, of NASA's Public Affairs Division, for providing information.

The photograph on the cover is an official NASA portrait of Eileen Collins, taken in 1999, the year she became the first woman commander of a space shuttle mission.

Contents

Some words are shown in bold, **like this.** You can find out what they mean by looking in the glossary.

Dreams of Flying

When she was a little girl, Eileen Collins dreamed of flying. But even in her wildest dreams she never imagined that one day she would become one of the most famous women pilots in history. On February 3, 1995, Collins became the first woman to fly the space shuttle. Four years later, on July 22, 1999, Collins became the first woman **commander** of a space shuttle mission.

In 1999 the shuttle *Columbia* blasted off with Eileen Collins in comman...

Commander

The commander is the leader, or person in charge, of the team of astronauts on a space shuttle mission. The commander flies the shuttle during approach and landing.

Timeline

1956	1978	1979	1980	1987
Born on November 19 in Elmira, New York	**Graduates** *from Syracuse University*	*Graduates from pilot training*	*Becomes first female flight instructor at Vance Air Force Base*	*Marries Pat Youngs*

Eileen Marie Collins was born in Elmira, New York, on November 19, 1956. As a young child, Eileen joined her parents, James and Rose Marie, her two brothers and her sister on trips to the Elmira-Corning airport to watch planes take off and land.

The Collins family lived near the Harris Hill Soaring Center where Eileen saw **gliders** sweep across the sky. She watched *Star Trek* on television, and dreamed of going into space.

Eileen Collins wears her orange launch suit in this **NASA** photo.

1990	1991	1995	2000	2005
Completes Air Force Test Pilot School	*Becomes an astronaut*	*Pilot of STS-63; daughter Bridget is born*	*Son Luke is born*	*Commander of the Return to Flight mission*

Early Heroes

When Eileen was nine, her parents separated. Her father changed jobs, and her mother tried to find work. Eileen's family was not rich. They could not afford airplane rides or flying lessons, but they always encouraged Eileen to work hard and dream big.

When she was in fourth grade, Eileen read a newspaper story about space exploration. Some experts said the country was wasting money exploring space. Eileen disagreed. She felt that exploring space was important.

This photograph is of Eileen Collins as a child.

Mercury 13

In 1961, thirteen women pilots passed the tests to become astronauts for the first space program, Project Mercury. The men who passed became astronauts and flew into space, but the women's program was cancelled.

In high school, Eileen read about the famous pilot Amelia Earhart and the women who served in World War II (1939–1945) by flying new airplanes from factories to military bases. When Eileen read about the space program, she wondered why there were no women astronauts.

Amelia Earhart (1898–1937) was a famous woman pilot.

Learning to Fly

When she was sixteen, Eileen got a job in a store and started saving money for flying lessons. When she **graduated** from high school in 1974, Eileen began classes at Corning Community College. She worked while in college and saved $1,000 toward flying lessons.

Eileen loved flying and learned quickly. When she took her first flight on her own, the airplane door popped open. Eileen remained calm and in control. She earned her pilot's license when she was twenty years old.

Eileen earned a college **degree** after two years at Corning.

Jerrie Cobb, one of the Mercury 13, was the first woman to pass all three astronaut tests in 1960.

Collins attended Syracuse University in Syracuse, New York, from 1976 through 1978.

Eileen won a **scholarship** to go to Syracuse University. In 1978, she graduated from Syracuse with a degree in math and economics.

The Air Force had begun accepting women into its pilot training program. Eileen applied. She was accepted along with one other woman and 35 men.

Air Force Pilot

Collins began pilot training at Vance Air Force Base in Oklahoma. During that time, the first six women astronauts arrived for parachute training. As Collins watched them train, she realized that her childhood dream of becoming an astronaut might be possible.

The first step was completing her pilot training. After she **graduated**, Collins stayed on as the first woman flight **instructor** at Vance Air Force Base.

NASA's first women astronauts were (from left) Rhea Seddon, Kathryn Sullivan, Judith Resnick, Sally Ride, Anna Fisher, and Shannon Lucid.

This C-141 is the kind of plane that Collins flew to Grenada.

When Collins first became an Air Force pilot, women were not allowed to fly fighter planes. That did not make any sense to Collins. She was as qualified as the male pilots.

Collins moved to Travis Air Force Base in California. By then, the rules about women pilots had changed. In 1983 Collins flew C-141 cargo jets carrying equipment and troops to a battlefield on the Caribbean island of Grenada.

Preparing for the Future

While she was a flight **instructor** in California, Collins met Pat Youngs. He was an instructor, too. They married in 1987. The couple moved to Colorado, where Collins taught math and trained pilots at the Air Force Academy.

Collins practiced emergency ejections from an aircraft during her Air Force survival course.

In 1986 and 1989, Collins earned two more degrees in space science. She hoped her education would help her to become an astronaut.

Eileen Collins was the first woman to:

- *Become a flight instructor at Vance Air Force Base*
- *Pilot the space shuttle*
- *Command a space shuttle mission*
- ***Dock** the space shuttle with the International Space Station.*

When Collins was 32, she became the second woman pilot ever accepted into the Air Force Test Pilot School at Edwards Air Force Base. While she was attending test pilot school, she heard that **NASA** was looking for astronauts. Collins applied to the space program. She finished test pilot school and began astronaut training in the same year.

Women Astronauts

Many women had been **mission specialists**, *scientists who performed experiments and helped with the equipment. No woman had ever flown the shuttle until Eileen Collins did so.*

Here Collins is standing in front of a T-38 jet at test pilot school.

Training for Space Flight

Collins reported to the Johnson Space Center in Texas for astronaut training. She spent most of her time learning about the space shuttle. She also studied the history of the space program, **astronomy**, weather, and medicine.

Survival training taught Collins and the other astronaut candidates how to stay alive in the wilderness and how to parachute from airplanes. Collins enjoyed the classes and felt ready to fly in outer space.

The astronaut in this picture is practicing for an emergency water landing after ejecting from an aircraft.

Collins trained for space flights in a simulator.

The hardest part of the training was working in a **simulator,** or model, of a space vehicle. As Collins sat in the simulator pretending to fly the shuttle, the trainers created problems that she and her crew had to solve. Sometimes they set up the simulator so that twenty different problems happened at once. Collins had to figure out what was wrong, fix it, and move to the next problem. She later said that the difficult training prepared her well for space flight.

Assignments

The Johnson Space Center in Houston, Texas, is home to the astronauts.

In July 1991, Collins finished astronaut training. Like all astronauts, she was given several assignments while waiting for her first space flight. She worked with a team of astronauts and scientists helping prepare the equipment for shuttle missions. She also worked on the astronaut support team to check the shuttle before launch and to plan for the launch. She helped decide how the crew got into and out of the shuttle.

Collins took her turn as **capcom**, or spacecraft communicator. Only the capcom speaks directly to the crew on a regular basis.

She worked as an information officer and as safety chief. All of these jobs were important to the space program, but Collins was eager to fly her own mission. In 1994, she was selected to be the pilot on STS-63.

STS

Each shuttle flight is given an STS number. STS stands for Space Transportation System.

Here Collins stands with the crew of STS-93 during training in a **simulator**.

Shuttle Pilot, STS-63

Flight STS-63 was the 67th shuttle mission. Collins would be the pilot, second in command to astronaut James Wetherbee. STS-63 was the first flight of the new Russian-American Space Program. The space shuttle *Discovery* would **rendezvous** with, or meet, the Russian space station *Mir*. **NASA** hoped that the shuttle would be able to deliver people and supplies to *Mir*. The rendezvous was an important step in the **cooperation** between Russia and the United States in space.

The crew of STS-63 included (from left front) Janice Voss, Eileen Collins, James Wetherbee, Vladimir Titov, Bernard Harris, and Michael Foale.

This photo shows the Russian space station *Mir* flying over the Pacific Ocean.

STS-63's launch was held up by nine months. Collins used the time to learn Russian and to study *Mir*. She wanted to be ready for the rendezvous.

Finally, on February 3, 1995, the *Discovery* blasted into space with Collins in the pilot's seat. Both the Russians and NASA were concerned about some leaks in *Discovery*, but they talked about this and decided to go ahead. Collins and the crew steered the *Discovery* close to *Mir* and then flew around it. The mission was a success.

Return to Earth and Back to Space

After eight days in space, Collins landed the shuttle back on Earth. Everything had gone perfectly on STS-63. Many people, including the Mercury 13, cheered the first female shuttle pilot. Collins had traveled 2.9 million miles (4.7 million kilometers) during her 145 orbits of Earth.

This photo shows the *Discovery* preparing to dock with *Mir*.

Less than a year after returning from space, Collins gave birth to her first child, a daughter named Bridget. Sometimes the crew called Collins "Mom." Now she was a real mom.

Collins's second shuttle mission, STS-84, also involved the Russian space station *Mir*. The shuttle took off on May 15, 1997. Collins **docked**, or connected, with *Mir*.

The astronauts moved a total of 249 items weighing nearly 4 tons (3.6 metric tons) to *Mir*. This included equipment, supplies, and about 1,000 pounds (454 kilograms) of water for the people living on *Mir*. They also left astronaut Michael Foale on *Mir* and brought home astronaut Jerry Linenger. Nine days after takeoff, Collins and the crew guided the shuttle back to Earth.

During the STS-84 mission, Collins flew the *Atlantis*, shown here landing in Florida.

Commander, STS-93

On both STS-63 and STS-84, Collins had been the pilot and second in command. On STS-93, she became the first woman to serve as the shuttle **commander**. Before the flight, Collins spent hundreds of hours in the **simulator**. She was determined to make the mission a success.

On July 22, 1999, the space shuttle *Columbia* lifted off. The purpose of the five-day mission was to put the *Chandra* **X-Ray Observatory** into **orbit**.

STS-93 lifted off at 11:30 at night on July 22, 1999.

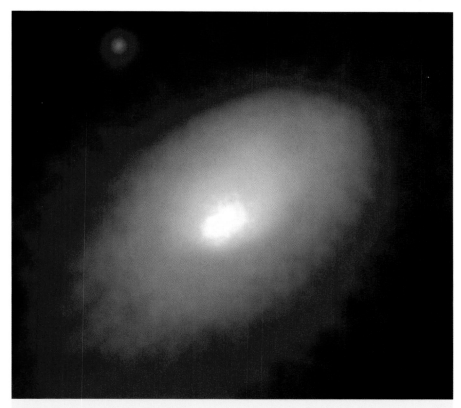

This photo of the galaxy was taken by the *Chandra* X-Ray Observatory.

Five seconds after the *Columbia* lifted off, Collins noticed a problem. A wire short-circuited and knocked out two of the shuttle's six computers. A pin came loose and damaged tubes in the engine. Fuel leaked out and the engines shut down early. The space shuttle stopped 7 miles (11 kilometers) short of its target. All the hours of training paid off. Collins and her crew were able to fix the problems, and the mission continued.

Launching *Chandra*

Launching the *Chandra* **X-Ray Observatory** into **orbit** was the most important part of the mission.

Chandra weighs 5 tons (4.5 metric tons) and orbits 40,000 miles (64,000 kilometers) above Earth. It takes pictures of exploding stars, **quasars,** and distant planets.

Chandra

The Chandra Observatory was named for an Indian-American **astrophysicist** *known as Chandra. He won a Nobel Prize in 1983 for his work on stars and is one of the most important scientists of the 20th century.*

Here the STS-93 crew members hold a model of *Chandra*, the world's most powerful X-ray **telescope**.

Once *Chandra* was placed in orbit, the crew worked on other experiments. They studied how plants grow in space and tried to contact short-wave radio operators on Earth. They also took pictures of Earth from space. On July 27, 1999, the shuttle returned to Kennedy Space Center in Florida. The mission was a success.

In 2000, Collins took a break from work to give birth to her son, Luke. Then she began preparing for her fourth shuttle mission, STS-114.

Collins was happy to see her daughter after the flight of STS-93.

STS-114

On February 1, 2003, Collins was watching television when she saw the space shuttle *Columbia* break up during its re-entry from space. She was stunned. The seven astronauts on board were her friends.

Collins had been preparing for her next flight, STS-114, but everything stopped while the scientists at **NASA** tried to figure out why the *Columbia* exploded. They discovered that a hole in the heat shield allowed hot gases to damage the shuttle.

The STS-114 mission patch is shown at the front of this photo of Collins and the crew.

Collins and the crew of STS-114 were given a new mission. This mission, called the Return to Flight, would focus on shuttle safety. They spent months going over safety procedures. They practiced repairing the shuttle in space.

After many delays, STS-114 made a perfect liftoff on July 26, 2005, at 10:39 A.M. The shuttle traveled to the International Space Station. The shuttle was loaded with supplies for the space station astronauts.

A camera on the launch pad recorded the space shuttle *Discovery* taking off on the historic Return to Flight mission STS-114.

Return to Flight

Once they reached the space station, it was time to find out if the shuttle had been damaged on liftoff. Collins took over as pilot. She flipped the shuttle onto its back so that cameras on the space station could check for loose tiles or other problems. They discovered a problem.

Collins and the **NASA** scientists decided to make repairs. Astronaut Steve Robinson put on his space suit. He stood on the robotic arm of the International Space Station and fixed the shuttle's tiles.

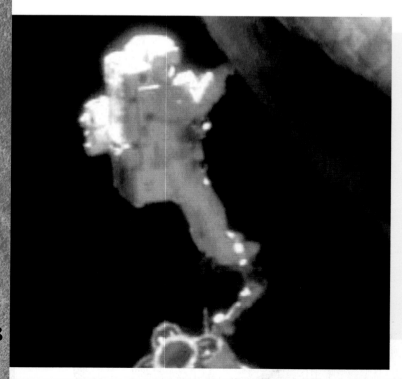

A camera attached to *Discovery*'s robotic arm shows astronaut Steve Robinson repairing the underside of the shuttle. No one had ever tried anything like this before.

On August 9, 2005, Collins guided the *Discovery* to a perfect landing in California. Collins and the STS-114 crew made history when they repaired the shuttle in space.

Whether Collins returns to space or stays on Earth teaching others, she will encourage girls or boys to study math and science and to support space exploration. She looks forward to the day when astronauts will explore the planet Mars.

Everyone at NASA and around the world was glad when *Discovery* landed safely. Here managers from NASA greet Commander Eileen Collins and the crew of STS-114.

Glossary

astronomy   study of stars

astrophysicist   scientist who studies the stars, galaxies, and space

capcom   person who talks to the crew during a shuttle mission

commander   person in charge

cooperation   working together

degree   rank given by a college for completing studies

dock   meet in space

glider   airplane without an engine that flies using air currents

graduate   complete school

instructor   teacher

mission specialist   astronaut who performs experiments and helps with equipment

NASA   National Aeronautics and Space Administration, the agency that studies and carries out work in space

observatory   structure used to allow people to watch stars

orbit   move in a circle around something

quasar   distant, powerful, star-like object

rendezvous   [RON • day • voo] when two vehicles meet in space

scholarship   money to pay for school

simulator   model of a space vehicle used in training

telescope   instrument that makes the stars seem nearer

X-ray   wave of energy that travels through soft materials

More Books to Read

Branley, Franklyn M. *The International Space Station.* New York: HarperCollins, 2000.

Goldsmith, Mike. *Space Travel.* Austin: Raintree Steck-Vaughn, 2001.

Lassieur, Allison. *The Space Shuttle.* New York: Children's Press, 2000.

Shearer, Deborah S. *Astronauts at Work.* Mankato, Minn.: Bridgestone Books, 2002.

Places to Visit

National Soaring Museum
Harris Hill
Elmira, New York 14903
Phone: (607) 734-3128

Kids Space Place
Space Center Houston
1601 NASA Parkway (formerly NASA Rd 1)
Houston, Texas 77058
Visitor Information: (281) 244-2100

Kennedy Space Center Visitor Complex
Route 405
Orsino, Florida 32899
Visitor Information: (321) 449-4444

Index